THIS PLANNER BELONGS TO

MISSION POSSIBLE

WEEKLY PLANNER

WATERBROOK

HELLO!

I am so glad you picked up this planner! That action means you want to take one more intentional step to living mission possible! If you haven't had a chance to read my book *Mission Possible*, let me share with you a bit about why I'm so passionate about this.

Living a mission-possible life means executing the good works that God has already prepared for you to do. We can achieve this because of what Jesus did for us on the cross more than two thousand years ago. With the sacrifice He made and His power to trample over death, He equips us and walks with us as we live this kind of life. It's a life that counts because of what God has done and is doing through you.

We are each on a mission to make a difference—to help the hurting, to reach the last, the lost, and the least. It looks different for everyone. It might take you on a rescue mission across the globe. It might keep you home in your neighborhood, breathing life and spirit into your children or neighbors. When you are mission-driven, you use your ability and God's empowerment to help, serve, guide, teach, pray, and lead others in innumerable ways as unique as each person's DNA.

I believe Scripture gives us one shared and large purpose, which is to glorify God. As believers, we honor and serve him with our lives, our natural gifts, our resources, our bodies, our worship, our decisions—the list is vast. If you've been a believer long enough, you have probably heard of the Great Commission. In Jesus's last instructions to His disciples, He commanded them to "Go, therefore, and make disciples of all the nations, baptizing them in the name of the Father and the Son and the Holy Spirit, teaching them to follow all that I commanded you; and behold, I am with you always, to the end of the age" (Matthew 28:19–20). I like to think of this command as marching orders for the church.

Within that great purpose of glorifying God, we find our purpose in what we do every day—which is all about being mission-driven in our ordinary lives.

Let's take the first step, together, to living mission possible.

TIM TEBOW

A MISSION-POSSIBLE LIFE IS POSSIBLE!

HOW TO USE THIS PLANNER

Within the first few pages of this planner, you are invited to write your own mission statement. Helpful questions and examples will prompt you to think through it. Having a mission statement will keep you focused and guide you the rest of the year as you work through your goals.

Since this planner is designed to be used any time of year, it's undated, so you'll want to write out the dates, using the yearly calendar guides that are on pages 4–5.

At the beginning of each month, there is room for you to reflect on the past month and set goals for the coming month. The hope is that by looking back, you'll be encouraged as you see your wins, which will help you reach your goals each month. And by spending some time planning ahead, you'll also be able to stay on track and reset periodically.

Each month and week also has an inspirational quote from *Mission Possible* and God's Word to keep you motivated.

By using this planner as a resource and source of encouragement, you can stay on track and reach the goals of your mission-possible life!

2022

JANUARY
S M T W T F S
. 1
2 3 4 5 6 7 8
9 10 11 12 13 14 15
16 17 18 19 20 21 22
23 24 25 26 27 28 29
30 31

FEBRUARY
S M T W T F S
. . 1 2 3 4 5
6 7 8 9 10 11 12
13 14 15 16 17 18 19
20 21 22 23 24 25 26
27 28

MARCH
S M T W T F S
. . 1 2 3 4 5
6 7 8 9 10 11 12
13 14 15 16 17 18 19
20 21 22 23 24 25 26
27 28 29 30 31

APRIL
S M T W T F S
. . . . . 1 2
3 4 5 6 7 8 9
10 11 12 13 14 15 16
17 18 19 20 21 22 23
24 25 26 27 28 29 30

MAY
S M T W T F S
1 2 3 4 5 6 7
8 9 10 11 12 13 14
15 16 17 18 19 20 21
22 23 24 25 26 27 28
29 30

JUNE
S M T W T F S
. . . 1 2 3 4
5 6 7 8 9 10 11
12 13 14 15 16 17 18
19 20 21 22 23 24 25
26 27 28 29 30

JULY
S M T W T F S
. . . . . 1 2
3 4 5 6 7 8 9
10 11 12 13 14 15 16
17 18 19 20 21 22 23
24 25 26 27 28 29 30
31

AUGUST
S M T W T F S
. 1 2 3 4 5 6
7 8 9 10 11 12 13
14 15 16 17 18 19 20
21 22 23 24 25 26 27
28 29 30 31

SEPTEMBER
S M T W T F S
. . . . 1 2
3 4 5 6 7 8 9
10 11 12 13 14 15 16
17 18 19 20 21 22 23
24 25 26 27 28 29 30

OCTOBER
S M T W T F S
. 1
2 3 4 5 6 7 8
9 10 11 12 13 14 15
16 17 18 19 20 21 22
23 24 25 26 27 28 29
30 31

NOVEMBER
S M T W T F S
. . 1 2 3 4 5
6 7 8 9 10 11 12
13 14 15 16 17 18 19
20 21 22 23 24 25 26
27 28 29 30

DECEMBER
S M T W T F S
. . . . 1 2 3
4 5 6 7 8 9 10
11 12 13 14 15 16 17
18 19 20 21 22 23 24
25 26 27 28 29 30 31

2023

JANUARY
S M T W T F S
1 2 3 4 5 6 7
8 9 10 11 12 13 14
15 16 17 18 19 20 21
22 23 24 25 26 27 28
29 30 31

FEBRUARY
S M T W T F S
. . . 1 2 3 4
5 6 7 8 9 10 11
12 13 14 15 16 17 18
19 20 21 22 23 24 25
26 27 28

MARCH
S M T W T F S
. . . 1 2 3 4
5 6 7 8 9 10 11
12 13 14 15 16 17 18
19 20 21 22 23 24 25
26 27 28 29 30 31

APRIL
S M T W T F S
. 1
2 3 4 5 6 7 8
9 10 11 12 13 14 15
16 17 18 19 20 21 22
23 24 25 26 27 28 29
30

MAY
S M T W T F S
. 1 2 3 4 5 6
7 8 9 10 11 12 13
14 15 16 17 18 19 20
21 22 23 24 25 26 27
28 29 30 31

JUNE
S M T W T F S
. . . . 1 2 3
4 5 6 7 8 9 10
11 12 13 14 15 16 17
18 19 20 21 22 23 24
25 26 27 28 29 30

JULY
S M T W T F S
. 1
2 3 4 5 6 7 8
9 10 11 12 13 14 15
16 17 18 19 20 21 22
23 24 25 26 27 28 29
30 31

AUGUST
S M T W T F S
. . 1 2 3 4 5
6 7 8 9 10 11 12
13 14 15 16 17 18 19
20 21 22 23 24 25 26
27 28 29 30 31

SEPTEMBER
S M T W T F S
. . . . . 1 2
3 4 5 6 7 8 9
10 11 12 13 14 15 16
17 18 19 20 21 22 23
24 25 26 27 28 29 30

OCTOBER
S M T W T F S
1 2 3 4 5 6 7
8 9 10 11 12 13 14
15 16 17 18 19 20 21
22 23 24 25 26 27 28
29 30 31

NOVEMBER
S M T W T F S
. . . 1 2 3 4
5 6 7 8 9 10 11
12 13 14 15 16 17 18
19 20 21 22 23 24 25
26 27 28 29 30

DECEMBER
S M T W T F S
. . . . . 1 2
3 4 5 6 7 8 9
10 11 12 13 14 15 16
17 18 19 20 21 22 23
24 25 26 27 28 29 30
31

2024

JANUARY
S M T W T F S
. 1 2 3 4 5 6
7 8 9 10 11 12 13
14 15 16 17 18 19 20
21 22 23 24 25 26 27
28 29 30 31

FEBRUARY
S M T W T F S
. . . . 1 2 3
4 5 6 7 8 9 10
11 12 13 14 15 16 17
18 19 20 21 22 23 24
25 26 27 28 29

MARCH
S M T W T F S
. . . . . 1 2
3 4 5 6 7 8 9
10 11 12 13 14 15 16
17 18 19 20 21 22 23
24 25 26 27 28 29 30
31

APRIL
S M T W T F S
. 1 2 3 4 5 6
7 8 9 10 11 12 13
14 15 16 17 18 19 20
21 22 23 24 25 26 27
28 29 30

MAY
S M T W T F S
. . . 1 2 3 4
5 6 7 8 9 10 11
12 13 14 15 16 17 18
19 20 21 22 23 24 25
26 27 28 29 30 31

JUNE
S M T W T F S
. 1
2 3 4 5 6 7 8
9 10 11 12 13 14 15
16 17 18 19 20 21 22
23 24 25 26 27 28 29
30

JULY
S M T W T F S
. 1 2 3 4 5 6
7 8 9 10 11 12 13
14 15 16 17 18 19 20
21 22 23 24 25 26 27
28 29 30 31

AUGUST
S M T W T F S
. . . . 1 2 3
4 5 6 7 8 9 10
11 12 13 14 15 16 17
18 19 20 21 22 23 24
25 26 27 28 29 30 31

SEPTEMBER
S M T W T F S
1 2 3 4 5 6 7
8 9 10 11 12 13 14
15 16 17 18 19 20 21
22 23 24 25 26 27 28
29 30

OCTOBER
S M T W T F S
. . 1 2 3 4 5
6 7 8 9 10 11 12
13 14 15 16 17 18 19
20 21 22 23 24 25 26
27 28 29 30 31

NOVEMBER
S M T W T F S
. . . . . 1 2
3 4 5 6 7 8 9
10 11 12 13 14 15 16
17 18 19 20 21 22 23
24 25 26 27 28 29 30

DECEMBER
S M T W T F S
1 2 3 4 5 6 7
8 9 10 11 12 13 14
15 16 17 18 19 20 21
22 23 24 25 26 27 28
29 30 31

2025

JANUARY
S	M	T	W	T	F	S
			1	2	3	4
5	6	7	8	9	10	11
12	13	14	15	16	17	18
19	20	21	22	23	24	25
26	27	28	29	30	31	

FEBRUARY
S	M	T	W	T	F	S
						1
2	3	4	5	6	7	8
9	10	11	12	13	14	15
16	17	18	19	20	21	22
23	24	25	26	27	28	

MARCH
S	M	T	W	T	F	S
						1
2	3	4	5	6	7	8
9	10	11	12	13	14	15
16	17	18	19	20	21	22
23	24	25	26	27	28	29
30	31					

APRIL
S	M	T	W	T	F	S
		1	2	3	4	5
6	7	8	9	10	11	12
13	14	15	16	17	18	19
20	21	22	23	24	25	26
27	28	29	30			

MAY
S	M	T	W	T	F	S
				1	2	3
4	5	6	7	8	9	10
11	12	13	14	15	16	17
18	19	20	21	22	23	24
25	26	27	28	29	30	31

JUNE
S	M	T	W	T	F	S
1	2	3	4	5	6	7
8	9	10	11	12	13	14
15	16	17	18	19	20	21
22	23	24	25	26	27	28
29	30					

JULY
S	M	T	W	T	F	S
		1	2	3	4	5
6	7	8	9	10	11	12
13	14	15	16	17	18	19
20	21	22	23	24	25	26
27	28	29	30	31		

AUGUST
S	M	T	W	T	F	S
					1	2
3	4	5	6	7	8	9
10	11	12	13	14	15	16
17	18	19	20	21	22	23
24	25	26	27	28	29	30
31						

SEPTEMBER
S	M	T	W	T	F	S
	1	2	3	4	5	6
7	8	9	10	11	12	13
14	15	16	17	18	19	20
21	22	23	24	25	26	27
28	29	30				

OCTOBER
S	M	T	W	T	F	S
			1	2	3	4
5	6	7	8	9	10	11
12	13	14	15	16	17	18
19	20	21	22	23	24	25
26	27	28	29	30	31	

NOVEMBER
S	M	T	W	T	F	S
						1
2	3	4	5	6	7	8
9	10	11	12	13	14	15
16	17	18	19	20	21	22
23	24	25	26	27	28	29
30						

DECEMBER
S	M	T	W	T	F	S
	1	2	3	4	5	6
7	8	9	10	11	12	13
14	15	16	17	18	19	20
21	22	23	24	25	26	27
28	29	30	31			

2026

JANUARY
S	M	T	W	T	F	S
				1	2	3
4	5	6	7	8	9	10
11	12	13	14	15	16	17
18	19	20	21	22	23	24
25	26	27	28	29	30	31

FEBRUARY
S	M	T	W	T	F	S
1	2	3	4	5	6	7
8	9	10	11	12	13	14
15	16	17	18	19	20	21
22	23	24	25	26	27	28

MARCH
S	M	T	W	T	F	S
1	2	3	4	5	6	7
8	9	10	11	12	13	14
15	16	17	18	19	20	21
22	23	24	25	26	27	28
29	30	31				

APRIL
S	M	T	W	T	F	S
			1	2	3	4
5	6	7	8	9	10	11
12	13	14	15	16	17	18
19	20	21	22	23	24	25
26	27	28	29	30		

MAY
S	M	T	W	T	F	S
					1	2
3	4	5	6	7	8	9
10	11	12	13	14	15	16
17	18	19	20	21	22	23
24	25	26	27	28	29	30
31						

JUNE
S	M	T	W	T	F	S
	1	2	3	4	5	6
7	8	9	10	11	12	13
14	15	16	17	18	19	20
21	22	23	24	25	26	27
28	29	30				

JULY
S	M	T	W	T	F	S
			1	2	3	4
5	6	7	8	9	10	11
12	13	14	15	16	17	18
19	20	21	22	23	24	25
26	27	28	29	30	31	

AUGUST
S	M	T	W	T	F	S
						1
2	3	4	5	6	7	8
9	10	11	12	13	14	15
16	17	18	19	20	21	22
23	24	25	26	27	28	29
30	31					

SEPTEMBER
S	M	T	W	T	F	S
		1	2	3	4	5
6	7	8	9	10	11	12
13	14	15	16	17	18	19
20	21	22	23	24	25	26
27	28	29	30			

OCTOBER
S	M	T	W	T	F	S
				1	2	3
4	5	6	7	8	9	10
11	12	13	14	15	16	17
18	19	20	21	22	23	24
25	26	27	28	29	30	31

NOVEMBER
S	M	T	W	T	F	S
1	2	3	4	5	6	7
8	9	10	11	12	13	14
15	16	17	18	19	20	21
22	23	24	25	26	27	28
29	30					

DECEMBER
S	M	T	W	T	F	S
		1	2	3	4	5
6	7	8	9	10	11	12
13	14	15	16	17	18	19
20	21	22	23	24	25	26
27	28	29	30	31		

2027

JANUARY
S	M	T	W	T	F	S
					1	2
3	4	5	6	7	8	9
10	11	12	13	14	15	16
17	18	19	20	21	22	23
24	25	26	27	28	29	30
31						

FEBRUARY
S	M	T	W	T	F	S
	1	2	3	4	5	6
7	8	9	10	11	12	13
14	15	16	17	18	19	20
21	22	23	24	25	26	27
28						

MARCH
S	M	T	W	T	F	S
	1	2	3	4	5	6
7	8	9	10	11	12	13
14	15	16	17	18	19	20
21	22	23	24	25	26	27
28	29	30	31			

APRIL
S	M	T	W	T	F	S
				1	2	3
4	5	6	7	8	9	10
11	12	13	14	15	16	17
18	19	20	21	22	23	24
25	26	27	28	29	30	

MAY
S	M	T	W	T	F	S
						1
2	3	4	5	6	7	8
9	10	11	12	13	14	15
16	17	18	19	20	21	22
23	24	25	26	27	28	29
30	31					

JUNE
S	M	T	W	T	F	S
		1	2	3	4	5
6	7	8	9	10	11	12
13	14	15	16	17	18	19
20	21	22	23	24	25	26
27	28	29	30			

JULY
S	M	T	W	T	F	S
				1	2	3
4	5	6	7	8	9	10
11	12	13	14	15	16	17
18	19	20	21	22	23	24
25	26	27	28	29	30	31

AUGUST
S	M	T	W	T	F	S
1	2	3	4	5	6	7
8	9	10	11	12	13	14
15	16	17	18	19	20	21
22	23	24	25	26	27	28
29	30	31				

SEPTEMBER
S	M	T	W	T	F	S
			1	2	3	4
5	6	7	8	9	10	11
12	13	14	15	16	17	18
19	20	21	22	23	24	25
26	27	28	29	30		

OCTOBER
S	M	T	W	T	F	S
					1	2
3	4	5	6	7	8	9
10	11	12	13	14	15	16
17	18	19	20	21	22	23
24	25	26	27	28	29	30
31						

NOVEMBER
S	M	T	W	T	F	S
	1	2	3	4	5	6
7	8	9	10	11	12	13
14	15	16	17	18	19	20
21	22	23	24	25	26	27
28	29	30				

DECEMBER
S	M	T	W	T	F	S
			1	2	3	4
5	6	7	8	9	10	11
12	13	14	15	16	17	18
19	20	21	22	23	24	25
26	27	28	29	30	31	

DEVELOPING YOUR MISSION STATEMENT

To cultivate a mission-possible life, form a mission statement that will help you stay focused and take action. Your personal mission statement will effectively:

- PROVIDE A FRAMEWORK FOR HOW YOU WANT TO LIVE
- EXPRESS YOUR VALUES AND PRIORITIES
- DETERMINE YOUR BEST SELF
- MOTIVATE YOU TO STAY THE COURSE

First, answer the following questions to help you think through what's important to you and fundamental to your mission statement:

WHAT IS YOUR PURPOSE AS A CHILD OF GOD?

_____

_____

_____

_____

_____

_____

WHAT LEGACY DO YOU WANT TO LEAVE?

_____

_____

_____

_____

_____

_____

WHAT DO YOU VALUE?

_____

_____

_____

_____

_____

WHO DO YOU WANT TO HELP AND HOW?

_____

_____

_____

_____

_____

Now you're ready to write out your mission statement! Here's the Tebow Foundation (and Tim Tebow's personal) mission statement as an example:

TO BRING FAITH, HOPE, AND LOVE TO THOSE NEEDING A BRIGHTER DAY IN THEIR DARKEST HOUR OF NEED.

MY MISSION STATEMENT:

"WHEN YOU BELIEVE THAT YOU ARE VALUABLE AND WORTHY BECAUSE OF WHO LIVES INSIDE YOU, EVERYTHING CHANGES."

TIM TEBOW

MY MISSION BOARD

Draw or paste pictures, words, or images to describe your mission-possible life.

MY MISSION BOARD

Draw or paste pictures, words, or images to describe your mission-possible life.

"WE ARE MOTIVATED NOT BY WHAT OTHERS THINK ABOUT US BUT BY HOW GOD SEES US. WE MAKE A DIFFERENCE NOT BY WHAT WE WEAR OR WHAT WE OWN BUT BY LIVING OUT EACH DAY IN A WAY THAT BRINGS GLORY TO HIM."

GOALS FOR THE UPCOMING MONTH

_____
_____
_____
_____
_____

3 THINGS I WILL DO

TO WORK TOWARD ACCOMPLISHING THE GOALS:

1 _____

_____

_____

2 _____

_____

_____

3 _____

_____

_____

_____
_____
_____
_____
_____

A PROMISE OF GOD

I WANT TO FOCUS ON THIS MONTH:

_____
_____
_____
_____
_____
_____
_____
_____
_____
_____

"

For God so loved the world that he gave his one and only Son, that whoever
believes in him shall not perish but have eternal life. —JOHN 3:16 (NIV)

MONTH

SUNDAY	MONDAY	TUESDAY

WEDNESDAY	THURSDAY	FRIDAY	SATURDAY

WEEK OF

ACTION STEPS FOR MY MISSION

○ _____

_____

_____

○ _____

_____

_____

○ _____

_____

_____

○ _____

_____

MONDAY _____

TUESDAY _____

WEDNESDAY _____

As believers, we honor and serve him with our lives, our natural gifts, our resources, our bodies, our worship, our decisions.

THURSDAY _____

FRIDAY _____

SATURDAY/SUNDAY _____

TO-DO LIST

○ _____
○ _____
○ _____
○ _____
○ _____
○ _____
○ _____
○ _____
○ _____
○ _____
○ _____
○ _____
○ _____
○ _____
○ _____
○ _____
○ _____
○ _____
○ _____
○ _____
○ _____

VERSE OF THE WEEK

ACTION STEPS FOR MY MISSION

○ _____

_____

○ _____

_____

○ _____

_____

○ _____

_____

MONDAY _____

TUESDAY _____

WEDNESDAY _____

Wherever you are and in whatever you do, not only can you find meaning but you can accomplish a mission that you have already been called to and equipped for.

THURSDAY _____

FRIDAY _____

SATURDAY/SUNDAY _____

○ _____
○ _____
○ _____
○ _____
○ _____
○ _____
○ _____
○ _____
○ _____
○ _____
○ _____
○ _____
○ _____
○ _____
○ _____
○ _____
○ _____
○ _____
○ _____
○ _____

WEEK OF

ACTION STEPS FOR MY MISSION

○ _____

_____

○ _____

_____

○ _____

_____

○ _____

_____

MONDAY _____

TUESDAY _____

WEDNESDAY _____

It's never too early or too late to start thinking about living a mission-possible life.

THURSDAY _____

FRIDAY _____

SATURDAY/SUNDAY _____

TO-DO LIST

- ○ _____
- ○ _____
- ○ _____
- ○ _____
- ○ _____
- ○ _____
- ○ _____
- ○ _____
- ○ _____
- ○ _____
- ○ _____
- ○ _____
- ○ _____
- ○ _____
- ○ _____
- ○ _____
- ○ _____
- ○ _____
- ○ _____

WEEK OF

MONDAY _____

ACTION STEPS FOR MY MISSION

○ _____

_____

○ _____

_____

○ _____

_____

○ _____

_____

TUESDAY _____

WEDNESDAY _____

Live with a greater significance than achievements, accolades, or an impressive bio.

TO-DO LIST

- ◯ _____
- ◯ _____
- ◯ _____
- ◯ _____
- ◯ _____
- ◯ _____
- ◯ _____
- ◯ _____
- ◯ _____
- ◯ _____
- ◯ _____
- ◯ _____
- ◯ _____
- ◯ _____
- ◯ _____
- ◯ _____
- ◯ _____
- ◯ _____
- ◯ _____
- ◯ _____
- ◯ _____

THURSDAY _____

FRIDAY _____

SATURDAY/SUNDAY _____

WEEK OF

MONDAY _____

TUESDAY _____

WEDNESDAY _____

ACTION STEPS FOR MY MISSION

○ _____

_____

○ _____

_____

○ _____

_____

○ _____

_____

The good news is that your mission is always possible when God is involved.

TO-DO LIST

THURSDAY _____

FRIDAY _____

SATURDAY/SUNDAY _____

○ _____
○ _____
○ _____
○ _____
○ _____
○ _____
○ _____
○ _____
○ _____
○ _____
○ _____
○ _____
○ _____
○ _____
○ _____
○ _____
○ _____
○ _____
○ _____
○ _____

REVIEWING THE PAST MONTH

WHAT WAS SUCCESSFUL THIS PAST MONTH:

MY WINS THIS PAST MONTH:

WHAT I DID THIS PAST MONTH TO FULFILL MY MISSION STATEMENT:

"YOU ARE IN THE RIGHT PLACE AT THE RIGHT TIME."

WHAT I WANT TO CONTINUE TO FOCUS ON NEXT MONTH:

HOW GOD SHOWED HIMSELF TO ME THIS PAST MONTH:

GOALS FOR THE UPCOMING MONTH

_____
_____
_____
_____
_____
_____

3 THINGS I WILL DO

TO WORK TOWARD ACCOMPLISHING THE GOALS:

1 _____

_____

_____

2 _____

_____

_____

3 _____

_____

_____

A PROMISE OF GOD

I WANT TO FOCUS ON THIS MONTH:

_____
_____
_____
_____
_____
_____
_____
_____
_____
_____

"

Come to me, all you who are weary and burdened, and I will give you rest.
Take my yoke upon you and learn from me, for I am gentle and humble in
heart, and you will find rest for your souls. — MATTHEW 11:28–29 (NIV)

MONTH

SUNDAY	MONDAY	TUESDAY

WEDNESDAY	THURSDAY	FRIDAY	SATURDAY

WEEK OF

MONDAY _____

TUESDAY _____

WEDNESDAY _____

ACTION STEPS FOR MY MISSION

○ _____

_____

○ _____

_____

○ _____

_____

○ _____

_____

If you are serving a God who has rattled the doors of hell and trampled over death, you can fulfill whatever He has called you to do.

THURSDAY _____

FRIDAY _____

SATURDAY/SUNDAY _____

○ _____
○ _____
○ _____
○ _____
○ _____
○ _____
○ _____
○ _____
○ _____
○ _____
○ _____
○ _____
○ _____
○ _____
○ _____
○ _____
○ _____
○ _____
○ _____
○ _____
○ _____

WEEK OF

ACTION STEPS FOR MY MISSION

○ _____

  _____

○ _____

  _____

○ _____

  _____

○ _____

  _____

MONDAY _____

TUESDAY _____

WEDNESDAY _____

Today you can begin to live your life on a trajectory that sets you up to accomplish feats of eternal purpose. Remember, with Him, all things are possible.

THURSDAY _____

FRIDAY _____

SATURDAY/SUNDAY _____

TO-DO LIST

- ○ _____
- ○ _____
- ○ _____
- ○ _____
- ○ _____
- ○ _____
- ○ _____
- ○ _____
- ○ _____
- ○ _____
- ○ _____
- ○ _____
- ○ _____
- ○ _____
- ○ _____
- ○ _____
- ○ _____
- ○ _____
- ○ _____
- ○ _____
- ○ _____

WEEK OF

ACTION STEPS FOR MY MISSION

○ _____

_____

○ _____

_____

○ _____

_____

○ _____

_____

MONDAY _____

TUESDAY _____

WEDNESDAY _____

When we choose to trust God with our lives, we have a sense of a higher calling.

THURSDAY _____

FRIDAY _____

SATURDAY/SUNDAY _____

WEEK OF

ACTION STEPS FOR MY MISSION

○ _____

_____

○ _____

_____

○ _____

_____

○ _____

_____

MONDAY _____

TUESDAY _____

WEDNESDAY _____

We are called to teach, care, love, help, pitch in, bear the burdens of others, and fight for those who can't fight for themselves.

THURSDAY _____

FRIDAY _____

SATURDAY/SUNDAY _____

○ _____
○ _____
○ _____
○ _____
○ _____
○ _____
○ _____
○ _____
○ _____
○ _____
○ _____
○ _____
○ _____
○ _____
○ _____
○ _____
○ _____
○ _____
○ _____
○ _____
○ _____

WEEK OF

MONDAY _____

TUESDAY _____

WEDNESDAY _____

ACTION STEPS FOR MY MISSION

○ _____

_____

_____

○ _____

_____

_____

○ _____

_____

_____

○ _____

_____

A mission-possible life has less to do with us and more to do with others.

THURSDAY _____

FRIDAY _____

SATURDAY/SUNDAY _____

TO-DO LIST

○ _____
○ _____
○ _____
○ _____
○ _____
○ _____
○ _____
○ _____
○ _____
○ _____
○ _____
○ _____
○ _____
○ _____
○ _____
○ _____
○ _____
○ _____
○ _____
○ _____

REVIEWING THE PAST MONTH

WHAT WAS SUCCESSFUL THIS PAST MONTH:

MY WINS THIS PAST MONTH:

WHAT I DID THIS PAST MONTH TO FULFILL MY MISSION STATEMENT:

"IT'S NOT YOUR STUFF GOD WANTS OR NEEDS; IT'S YOUR WILLINGNESS TO LIVE YOUR LIFE, EVERY PART OF IT, FOR HIM."

WHAT I WANT TO CONTINUE TO FOCUS ON NEXT MONTH:

HOW GOD SHOWED HIMSELF TO ME THIS PAST MONTH:

_____

_____

_____

_____

_____

3 THINGS I WILL DO

TO WORK TOWARD ACCOMPLISHING THE GOALS:

1 _____

_____

2 _____

_____

3 _____

_____

A PROMISE OF GOD

I WANT TO FOCUS ON THIS MONTH:

_____

_____

_____

_____

_____

_____

_____

_____

"

Now to Him who is able to do far more abundantly beyond all that we ask or think, according to the power that works within us. — EPHESIANS 3:20

MONTH

SUNDAY	MONDAY	TUESDAY

WEDNESDAY	THURSDAY	FRIDAY	SATURDAY

WEEK OF _____

ACTION STEPS FOR MY MISSION

○ _____

_____

○ _____

_____

○ _____

_____

○ _____

_____

MONDAY _____

TUESDAY _____

WEDNESDAY _____

If you've made the decision to trust God, He gives you the mission and makes it possible.

THURSDAY _____

FRIDAY _____

SATURDAY/SUNDAY _____

TO-DO LIST

○ _____
○ _____
○ _____
○ _____
○ _____
○ _____
○ _____
○ _____
○ _____
○ _____
○ _____
○ _____
○ _____
○ _____
○ _____
○ _____
○ _____
○ _____
○ _____
○ _____
○ _____

WEEK OF

ACTION STEPS FOR MY MISSION

○ _____

_____

_____

○ _____

_____

_____

○ _____

_____

_____

○ _____

_____

_____

MONDAY _____

TUESDAY _____

WEDNESDAY _____

Whenever you are forced to make a decision between purpose and preference, choose purpose. It'll win every time.

○ _____
○ _____
○ _____
○ _____
○ _____
○ _____
○ _____
○ _____
○ _____
○ _____
○ _____
○ _____
○ _____
○ _____
○ _____
○ _____
○ _____
○ _____
○ _____
○ _____

THURSDAY _____

FRIDAY _____

SATURDAY/SUNDAY _____

WEEK OF _____

MONDAY _____

TUESDAY _____

WEDNESDAY _____

ACTION STEPS FOR MY MISSION

○ _____

_____

_____

○ _____

_____

○ _____

_____

○ _____

_____

Does your life actually show a sense of urgency in what you believe?

THURSDAY _____

FRIDAY _____

SATURDAY/SUNDAY _____

TO-DO LIST

○ _____
○ _____
○ _____
○ _____
○ _____
○ _____
○ _____
○ _____
○ _____
○ _____
○ _____
○ _____
○ _____
○ _____
○ _____
○ _____
○ _____
○ _____
○ _____

WEEK OF _____

MONDAY _____

ACTION STEPS FOR MY MISSION

○ _____

_____

_____

○ _____

_____

_____

○ _____

_____

_____

○ _____

_____

_____

TUESDAY _____

WEDNESDAY _____

When you get tired or overwhelmed or uncertain, don't forget the moment God changed your life. . . . Don't forget the moment He challenged you to join the fight.

THURSDAY _____

FRIDAY _____

SATURDAY/SUNDAY _____

- ◯ _____
- ◯ _____
- ◯ _____
- ◯ _____
- ◯ _____
- ◯ _____
- ◯ _____
- ◯ _____
- ◯ _____
- ◯ _____
- ◯ _____
- ◯ _____
- ◯ _____
- ◯ _____
- ◯ _____
- ◯ _____
- ◯ _____
- ◯ _____
- ◯ _____
- ◯ _____
- ◯ _____

WEEK OF

ACTION STEPS FOR MY MISSION

○ _____

_____

○ _____

_____

○ _____

_____

○ _____

_____

MONDAY _____

TUESDAY _____

WEDNESDAY _____

God has a habit of making His presence known or intervening in impossible missions.

THURSDAY _____

FRIDAY _____

SATURDAY/SUNDAY _____

○ _____
○ _____
○ _____
○ _____
○ _____
○ _____
○ _____
○ _____
○ _____
○ _____
○ _____
○ _____
○ _____
○ _____
○ _____
○ _____
○ _____
○ _____
○ _____
○ _____
○ _____

REVIEWING THE PAST MONTH

WHAT WAS SUCCESSFUL THIS PAST MONTH:

MY WINS THIS PAST MONTH:

WHAT I DID THIS PAST MONTH TO
FULFILL MY MISSION STATEMENT:

"DON'T DISMISS AN IDEA OR A PROMPTING THAT WELLS IN YOUR SOUL. PAY ATTENTION TO IT, AND DO SOMETHING WITH IT."

WHAT I WANT TO CONTINUE TO FOCUS ON NEXT MONTH:

HOW GOD SHOWED HIMSELF TO ME THIS PAST MONTH:

GOALS FOR THE UPCOMING MONTH

_____

_____

_____

_____

_____

_____

3 THINGS I WILL DO

TO WORK TOWARD ACCOMPLISHING THE GOALS:

1 _____

_____

_____

2 _____

_____

_____

3 _____

_____

_____

A PROMISE OF GOD

I WANT TO FOCUS ON THIS MONTH:

_____

_____

_____

_____

_____

_____

_____

_____

_____

_____

"

These things I have spoken to you so that in Me you may have peace.
In the world you have tribulation, but take courage; I have overcome
the world. —JOHN 16:33

MONTH

SUNDAY	MONDAY	TUESDAY

WEDNESDAY	THURSDAY	FRIDAY	SATURDAY

WEEK OF

ACTION STEPS FOR MY MISSION

○ _____

○ _____

○ _____

○ _____

MONDAY _____

TUESDAY _____

WEDNESDAY _____

The anchor of the gospel rests in the truth that we cannot save ourselves by our pedigrees, good works, or impressive career histories.

THURSDAY _____

FRIDAY _____

SATURDAY/SUNDAY _____

TO-DO LIST

○ _____
○ _____
○ _____
○ _____
○ _____
○ _____
○ _____
○ _____
○ _____
○ _____
○ _____
○ _____
○ _____
○ _____
○ _____
○ _____
○ _____
○ _____
○ _____
○ _____
○ _____

WEEK OF _____

ACTION STEPS FOR MY MISSION

○ _____

_____

○ _____

_____

○ _____

_____

○ _____

_____

MONDAY _____

TUESDAY _____

WEDNESDAY _____

When we make the decision to trust Him with our lives, we are automatically seated at the table of the humanly impossible. It's not about what we can do, it's about what God can do through us.

THURSDAY _____

FRIDAY _____

SATURDAY/SUNDAY _____

○ _____
○ _____
○ _____
○ _____
○ _____
○ _____
○ _____
○ _____
○ _____
○ _____
○ _____
○ _____
○ _____
○ _____
○ _____
○ _____
○ _____
○ _____
○ _____
○ _____

WEEK OF _____

MONDAY _____

TUESDAY _____

ACTION STEPS FOR MY MISSION

○ _____

_____

_____

○ _____

_____

_____

○ _____

_____

_____

WEDNESDAY _____

○ _____

_____

_____

Even if you feel incapable or insufficient, God has everything you need so you can do what He has put on your heart.

TO-DO LIST

○ _____
○ _____
○ _____
○ _____
○ _____
○ _____
○ _____
○ _____
○ _____
○ _____
○ _____
○ _____
○ _____
○ _____
○ _____
○ _____
○ _____
○ _____
○ _____
○ _____

THURSDAY _____

FRIDAY _____

SATURDAY/SUNDAY _____

WEEK OF

MONDAY _____

ACTION STEPS FOR MY MISSION

○ _____

_____

○ _____

_____

○ _____

_____

○ _____

_____

TUESDAY _____

WEDNESDAY _____

Instead of feeling overwhelmed by what seems impossible, imagine being overwhelmed by the spirit of God. Shift your focus, even just a little bit.

TO-DO LIST

- ○ _____
- ○ _____
- ○ _____
- ○ _____
- ○ _____
- ○ _____
- ○ _____
- ○ _____
- ○ _____
- ○ _____
- ○ _____
- ○ _____
- ○ _____
- ○ _____
- ○ _____
- ○ _____
- ○ _____
- ○ _____
- ○ _____

THURSDAY _____

FRIDAY _____

SATURDAY/SUNDAY _____

WEEK OF

ACTION STEPS FOR MY MISSION

○ _____

_____

○ _____

_____

○ _____

_____

○ _____

_____

MONDAY _____

TUESDAY _____

WEDNESDAY _____

Trade the anxiety, the dread, or the pressure that weighs heavily on your heart for the refreshing truth that God breathes life into you.

THURSDAY _____

FRIDAY _____

SATURDAY/SUNDAY _____

TO-DO LIST

○ _____
○ _____
○ _____
○ _____
○ _____
○ _____
○ _____
○ _____
○ _____
○ _____
○ _____
○ _____
○ _____
○ _____
○ _____
○ _____
○ _____
○ _____
○ _____
○ _____
○ _____

REVIEWING THE PAST MONTH

WHAT WAS SUCCESSFUL THIS PAST MONTH:

MY WINS THIS PAST MONTH:

WHAT I DID THIS PAST MONTH TO
FULFILL MY MISSION STATEMENT:

"A LIFE OF SIGNIFICANCE IS STEEPED IN SACRIFICE."

WHAT I WANT TO CONTINUE TO FOCUS ON NEXT MONTH:

HOW GOD SHOWED HIMSELF TO ME THIS PAST MONTH:

GOALS FOR THE UPCOMING MONTH

_____

_____

_____

_____

_____

3 THINGS I WILL DO

TO WORK TOWARD ACCOMPLISHING THE GOALS:

1 _____

_____

_____

2 _____

_____

_____

3 _____

_____

_____

_____

A PROMISE OF GOD

I WANT TO FOCUS ON THIS MONTH:

_____

_____

_____

_____

_____

_____

_____

_____

_____

_____

66

For we are His creation, created in Christ Jesus for good works, which God
prepared ahead of time so that we should walk in them. —EPHESIANS 2:10 (HCSB)

MONTH

SUNDAY	MONDAY	TUESDAY

WEDNESDAY	THURSDAY	FRIDAY	SATURDAY

WEEK OF

ACTION STEPS FOR MY MISSION

○ _____

_____

○ _____

_____

○ _____

_____

○ _____

_____

MONDAY _____

TUESDAY _____

WEDNESDAY _____

Our mission is not to end all evil. . . . Our mission is to honor God as we make a difference wherever and however we can.

THURSDAY _____

FRIDAY _____

SATURDAY/SUNDAY _____

TO-DO LIST

○ _____
○ _____
○ _____
○ _____
○ _____
○ _____
○ _____
○ _____
○ _____
○ _____
○ _____
○ _____
○ _____
○ _____
○ _____
○ _____
○ _____
○ _____
○ _____
○ _____
○ _____

WEEK OF _____

ACTION STEPS FOR MY MISSION

○ _____

_____

_____

○ _____

_____

_____

○ _____

_____

_____

○ _____

_____

MONDAY _____

TUESDAY _____

WEDNESDAY _____

Living a mission-possible life is not about growing our self-confidence; it's about expanding our God-confidence.

TO-DO LIST

- ◯ _____
- ◯ _____
- ◯ _____
- ◯ _____
- ◯ _____
- ◯ _____
- ◯ _____
- ◯ _____
- ◯ _____
- ◯ _____
- ◯ _____
- ◯ _____
- ◯ _____
- ◯ _____
- ◯ _____
- ◯ _____
- ◯ _____
- ◯ _____
- ◯ _____

THURSDAY _____

FRIDAY _____

SATURDAY/SUNDAY _____

WEEK OF

MONDAY _____

TUESDAY _____

WEDNESDAY _____

ACTION STEPS FOR MY MISSION

○ _____

_____

○ _____

_____

○ _____

_____

○ _____

_____

Don't stop trusting Him when it's dark, dank, and smelly. . . . When your doubt begins to rumble, remember what God has done in the past.

THURSDAY _____

FRIDAY _____

SATURDAY/SUNDAY _____

TO-DO LIST

○ _____
○ _____
○ _____
○ _____
○ _____
○ _____
○ _____
○ _____
○ _____
○ _____
○ _____
○ _____
○ _____
○ _____
○ _____
○ _____
○ _____
○ _____
○ _____
○ _____

WEEK OF

MONDAY _____

TUESDAY _____

WEDNESDAY _____

ACTION STEPS FOR MY MISSION

○ _____

_____

○ _____

_____

○ _____

_____

○ _____

_____

Being a mission-possible Christian has less to do with holding a religious vocation and more to do with developing an intimate relationship with Jesus.

THURSDAY _____

FRIDAY _____

SATURDAY/SUNDAY _____

TO-DO LIST

○ _____
○ _____
○ _____
○ _____
○ _____
○ _____
○ _____
○ _____
○ _____
○ _____
○ _____
○ _____
○ _____
○ _____
○ _____
○ _____
○ _____
○ _____
○ _____
○ _____

WEEK OF

ACTION STEPS FOR MY MISSION

○ _____

_____

○ _____

_____

○ _____

_____

○ _____

_____

MONDAY _____

TUESDAY _____

WEDNESDAY _____

Mission stems from embracing our identity in Jesus.

THURSDAY _____

FRIDAY _____

SATURDAY/SUNDAY _____

TO-DO LIST

○ _____
○ _____
○ _____
○ _____
○ _____
○ _____
○ _____
○ _____
○ _____
○ _____
○ _____
○ _____
○ _____
○ _____
○ _____
○ _____
○ _____
○ _____
○ _____
○ _____

REVIEWING THE PAST MONTH

WHAT WAS SUCCESSFUL THIS PAST MONTH:

MY WINS THIS PAST MONTH:

WHAT I DID THIS PAST MONTH TO
FULFILL MY MISSION STATEMENT:

**"WE DON'T KNOW ALL THE
THINGS GOD IS DOING IN US,
THROUGH US, BY US, OR AROUND US,
BUT WE GET TO TRUST THAT
HE LOVES US, BECAUSE HE
DEMONSTRATED IT."**

WHAT I WANT TO CONTINUE TO FOCUS ON NEXT MONTH:

HOW GOD SHOWED HIMSELF TO ME THIS PAST MONTH:

_____
_____
_____
_____
_____
_____

3 THINGS I WILL DO

TO WORK TOWARD ACCOMPLISHING THE GOALS:

1 _____
_____
_____

2 _____
_____
_____

3 _____
_____
_____

A PROMISE OF GOD

I WANT TO FOCUS ON THIS MONTH:

_____
_____
_____
_____
_____
_____
_____
_____
_____
_____

"

Go, therefore, and make disciples of all the nations, baptizing them in the name of the
Father and the Son and the Holy Spirit, teaching them to follow all that I commanded you;
and behold, I am with you always, to the end of the age. — MATTHEW 28:19–20

MONTH

SUNDAY	MONDAY	TUESDAY

WEDNESDAY	THURSDAY	FRIDAY	SATURDAY

WEEK OF _____

ACTION STEPS FOR MY MISSION

○ _____

_____

○ _____

_____

○ _____

_____

○ _____

_____

MONDAY _____

TUESDAY _____

WEDNESDAY _____

We are image bearers of God on the field, in the boardroom, and in our kitchens. Each minute. Each day. Every day.

TO-DO LIST

○ _____
○ _____
○ _____
○ _____
○ _____
○ _____
○ _____
○ _____
○ _____
○ _____
○ _____
○ _____
○ _____
○ _____
○ _____
○ _____
○ _____
○ _____
○ _____
○ _____
○ _____

THURSDAY _____

FRIDAY _____

SATURDAY/SUNDAY _____

WEEK OF

MONDAY _____

TUESDAY _____

WEDNESDAY _____

ACTION STEPS FOR MY MISSION

○ _____

_____

○ _____

_____

○ _____

_____

○ _____

_____

Living a mission-possible life means watering and fertilizing and cultivating the ground where you are planted, even if it seems nothing more than a wasteland.

THURSDAY _____

FRIDAY _____

SATURDAY/SUNDAY _____

TO-DO LIST

○ _____
○ _____
○ _____
○ _____
○ _____
○ _____
○ _____
○ _____
○ _____
○ _____
○ _____
○ _____
○ _____
○ _____
○ _____
○ _____
○ _____
○ _____
○ _____
○ _____

WEEK OF

ACTION STEPS FOR MY MISSION

○ _____

_____

○ _____

_____

○ _____

_____

○ _____

_____

MONDAY _____

TUESDAY _____

WEDNESDAY _____

Never overestimate what you can do by your own power, and never underestimate what God can do when you offer what you have and who you are fully to Him.

THURSDAY _____

FRIDAY _____

SATURDAY/SUNDAY _____

TO-DO LIST

○ _____
○ _____
○ _____
○ _____
○ _____
○ _____
○ _____
○ _____
○ _____
○ _____
○ _____
○ _____
○ _____
○ _____
○ _____
○ _____
○ _____
○ _____
○ _____
○ _____

WEEK OF

ACTION STEPS FOR MY MISSION

- ○ _____
- _____
- ○ _____
- _____
- ○ _____
- _____
- ○ _____
- _____

MONDAY _____

TUESDAY _____

WEDNESDAY _____

Today and tomorrow, we choose to cast and keep casting our cares on the One who brought us from death to life.

TO-DO LIST

○ _____
○ _____
○ _____
○ _____
○ _____
○ _____
○ _____
○ _____
○ _____
○ _____
○ _____
○ _____
○ _____
○ _____
○ _____
○ _____
○ _____
○ _____
○ _____
○ _____
○ _____

THURSDAY _____

FRIDAY _____

SATURDAY/SUNDAY _____

WEEK OF

ACTION STEPS FOR MY MISSION

○ _____

_____

○ _____

_____

○ _____

_____

○ _____

_____

MONDAY _____

TUESDAY _____

WEDNESDAY _____

Don't wait for purpose to find you some day. Say yes to what God says is possible for and through you in the present.

THURSDAY _____

FRIDAY _____

SATURDAY/SUNDAY _____

REVIEWING THE PAST MONTH

WHAT WAS SUCCESSFUL THIS PAST MONTH:

MY WINS THIS PAST MONTH:

WHAT I DID THIS PAST MONTH TO FULFILL MY MISSION STATEMENT:

> "YOU HAVE TO LIVE WITH
> OPEN EYES TO SEE THE NEEDS,
> AN OPEN HEART TO LOVE,
> AND OPEN HANDS TO SERVE."

WHAT I WANT TO CONTINUE TO FOCUS ON NEXT MONTH:

HOW GOD SHOWED HIMSELF TO ME THIS PAST MONTH:

_____

_____

_____

_____

_____

_____

3 THINGS I WILL DO

TO WORK TOWARD ACCOMPLISHING THE GOALS:

1 _____

_____

2 _____

_____

3 _____

_____

A PROMISE OF GOD

I WANT TO FOCUS ON THIS MONTH:

_____

_____

_____

_____

_____

_____

_____

_____

_____

Whatever you do, in word or in deed, do everything in the name of the Lord Jesus, giving thanks to God the Father through Him. — COLOSSIANS 3:17 (HCSB)

MONTH

	SUNDAY	MONDAY	TUESDAY

WEDNESDAY	THURSDAY	FRIDAY	SATURDAY

WEEK OF _____

ACTION STEPS FOR MY MISSION

○ _____

_____

○ _____

_____

○ _____

_____

○ _____

_____

MONDAY _____

TUESDAY _____

WEDNESDAY _____

Stick it out and fight for what you believe in when the glitz and glamour vanish and no one is watching.

TO-DO LIST

○ _____
○ _____
○ _____
○ _____
○ _____
○ _____
○ _____
○ _____
○ _____
○ _____
○ _____
○ _____
○ _____
○ _____
○ _____
○ _____
○ _____
○ _____
○ _____
○ _____
○ _____

THURSDAY _____

FRIDAY _____

SATURDAY/SUNDAY _____

WEEK OF

ACTION STEPS FOR MY MISSION

○ _____

_____

_____

○ _____

_____

○ _____

_____

○ _____

_____

MONDAY _____

TUESDAY _____

WEDNESDAY _____

Be faithful in what God is telling you to do. Do your part, pray and keep praying, and let God do His work.

THURSDAY _____

FRIDAY _____

SATURDAY/SUNDAY _____

TO-DO LIST

- ○ _____
- ○ _____
- ○ _____
- ○ _____
- ○ _____
- ○ _____
- ○ _____
- ○ _____
- ○ _____
- ○ _____
- ○ _____
- ○ _____
- ○ _____
- ○ _____
- ○ _____
- ○ _____
- ○ _____
- ○ _____
- ○ _____
- ○ _____
- ○ _____

WEEK OF

ACTION STEPS FOR MY MISSION

○ _____

_____

○ _____

_____

○ _____

_____

○ _____

_____

MONDAY _____

TUESDAY _____

WEDNESDAY _____

What can you do, starting now, to begin to live a mission-possible life?

TO-DO LIST

THURSDAY _____

FRIDAY _____

SATURDAY/SUNDAY _____

VERSE OF THE WEEK

WEEK OF _____

ACTION STEPS FOR MY MISSION

○ _____

_____

_____

○ _____

_____

_____

○ _____

_____

_____

○ _____

_____

MONDAY _____

TUESDAY _____

WEDNESDAY _____

Not only can great things come from the spark of an idea, but they can also be created by one person, one need, one problem, one issue.

TO-DO LIST

- ◯ _____
- ◯ _____
- ◯ _____
- ◯ _____
- ◯ _____
- ◯ _____
- ◯ _____
- ◯ _____
- ◯ _____
- ◯ _____
- ◯ _____
- ◯ _____
- ◯ _____
- ◯ _____
- ◯ _____
- ◯ _____
- ◯ _____
- ◯ _____
- ◯ _____
- ◯ _____

THURSDAY _____

FRIDAY _____

SATURDAY/SUNDAY _____

WEEK OF _____

ACTION STEPS FOR MY MISSION

○ _____

_____

○ _____

_____

○ _____

_____

○ _____

_____

MONDAY _____

TUESDAY _____

WEDNESDAY _____

Don't brush off something that seems small. . . .
It can change the world or even save a life.

TO-DO LIST

○ _____
○ _____
○ _____
○ _____
○ _____
○ _____
○ _____
○ _____
○ _____
○ _____
○ _____
○ _____
○ _____
○ _____
○ _____
○ _____
○ _____
○ _____
○ _____
○ _____
○ _____

THURSDAY _____

FRIDAY _____

SATURDAY/SUNDAY _____

REVIEWING THE PAST MONTH

WHAT WAS SUCCESSFUL THIS PAST MONTH:

MY WINS THIS PAST MONTH:

WHAT I DID THIS PAST MONTH TO
FULFILL MY MISSION STATEMENT:

"PURPOSE IS ALWAYS PRESENT, EVEN IN THE WAITING."

WHAT I WANT TO CONTINUE TO FOCUS ON NEXT MONTH:

HOW GOD SHOWED HIMSELF TO ME THIS PAST MONTH:

GOALS FOR THE UPCOMING MONTH

_____

_____

_____

_____

_____

_____

3 THINGS I WILL DO

TO WORK TOWARD ACCOMPLISHING THE GOALS:

1 _____

_____

_____

2 _____

_____

_____

3 _____

_____

A PROMISE OF GOD

I WANT TO FOCUS ON THIS MONTH:

_____

_____

_____

_____

_____

_____

_____

_____

_____

_____

"

This is my command—be strong and courageous! Do not be afraid or discouraged.
For the Lord your God is with you wherever you go. —JOSHUA 1:9 (NLT)

MONTH

SUNDAY	MONDAY	TUESDAY

WEDNESDAY	THURSDAY	FRIDAY	SATURDAY

WEEK OF _____

ACTION STEPS FOR MY MISSION

○ _____

_____

○ _____

_____

○ _____

_____

○ _____

_____

MONDAY _____

TUESDAY _____

WEDNESDAY _____

God can use you—yes, you!—to make a positive difference in the life of one or many.

TO-DO LIST

○ _____

○ _____

○ _____

○ _____

○ _____

○ _____

○ _____

○ _____

○ _____

○ _____

○ _____

○ _____

○ _____

○ _____

○ _____

○ _____

○ _____

○ _____

○ _____

○ _____

THURSDAY _____

FRIDAY _____

SATURDAY/SUNDAY _____

VERSE OF THE WEEK

ACTION STEPS FOR MY MISSION

○ _____

_____

_____

○ _____

_____

_____

○ _____

_____

_____

○ _____

_____

MONDAY _____

TUESDAY _____

WEDNESDAY _____

Once you spark movement, it will always lead to another opportunity, and another, and another after that. But it always starts with one step. Are you ready to take that step?

THURSDAY _____

FRIDAY _____

SATURDAY/SUNDAY _____

- ◯ _____
- ◯ _____
- ◯ _____
- ◯ _____
- ◯ _____
- ◯ _____
- ◯ _____
- ◯ _____
- ◯ _____
- ◯ _____
- ◯ _____
- ◯ _____
- ◯ _____
- ◯ _____
- ◯ _____
- ◯ _____
- ◯ _____
- ◯ _____
- ◯ _____
- ◯ _____

WEEK OF

MONDAY _____

ACTION STEPS FOR MY MISSION

○ _____

_____

_____

○ _____

_____

_____

○ _____

_____

_____

○ _____

_____

TUESDAY _____

WEDNESDAY _____

God loves to manifest miracles when we're vulnerable, when there are reasons we need them. It's usually when we've put ourselves in positions of discomfort on purpose.

TO-DO LIST

○ _____
○ _____
○ _____
○ _____
○ _____
○ _____
○ _____
○ _____
○ _____
○ _____
○ _____
○ _____
○ _____
○ _____
○ _____
○ _____
○ _____
○ _____
○ _____
○ _____
○ _____

THURSDAY _____

FRIDAY _____

SATURDAY/SUNDAY _____

VERSE OF THE WEEK

WEEK OF _____

ACTION STEPS FOR MY MISSION

○ _____

_____

_____

○ _____

_____

_____

○ _____

_____

_____

○ _____

_____

MONDAY _____

TUESDAY _____

WEDNESDAY _____

One of the greatest enemies of living a mission-possible life is the pursuit of comfort.

TO-DO LIST

○ _____
○ _____
○ _____
○ _____
○ _____
○ _____
○ _____
○ _____
○ _____
○ _____
○ _____
○ _____
○ _____
○ _____
○ _____
○ _____
○ _____
○ _____
○ _____
○ _____

THURSDAY _____

FRIDAY _____

SATURDAY/SUNDAY _____

WEEK OF

ACTION STEPS FOR MY MISSION

○ _____

_____

○ _____

_____

○ _____

_____

○ _____

_____

MONDAY _____

TUESDAY _____

WEDNESDAY _____

Don't run from the resistance. Remember, there is always a purpose to the pain.

TO-DO LIST

○ _____
○ _____
○ _____
○ _____
○ _____
○ _____
○ _____
○ _____
○ _____
○ _____
○ _____
○ _____
○ _____
○ _____
○ _____
○ _____
○ _____
○ _____
○ _____
○ _____

THURSDAY _____

FRIDAY _____

SATURDAY/SUNDAY _____

REVIEWING THE PAST MONTH

WHAT WAS SUCCESSFUL THIS PAST MONTH:

MY WINS THIS PAST MONTH:

WHAT I DID THIS PAST MONTH TO FULFILL MY MISSION STATEMENT:

"EVERY SINGLE ONE OF US HAS A CHANCE TO MAKE A DIFFERENCE. . . . IT'S MISSION POSSIBLE BECAUSE WE'VE TEAMED UP WITH THE GOD OF THIS UNIVERSE."

WHAT I WANT TO CONTINUE TO FOCUS ON NEXT MONTH:

HOW GOD SHOWED HIMSELF TO ME THIS PAST MONTH:

_____

_____

_____

_____

_____

_____

3 THINGS I WILL DO

TO WORK TOWARD ACCOMPLISHING THE GOALS:

1 _____

_____

2 _____

_____

3 _____

_____

A PROMISE OF GOD

I WANT TO FOCUS ON THIS MONTH:

_____

_____

_____

_____

_____

_____

_____

_____

_____

For we live by faith, not by sight. — 2 CORINTHIANS 5:7 (NIV)

MONTH

SUNDAY	MONDAY	TUESDAY

WEDNESDAY	THURSDAY	FRIDAY	SATURDAY

VERSE OF THE WEEK

ACTION STEPS FOR MY MISSION

○ _____

_____

_____

○ _____

_____

_____

○ _____

_____

_____

○ _____

_____

_____

WEEK OF _____

MONDAY _____

TUESDAY _____

WEDNESDAY _____

While emotions may be telltale signs of whatever we are facing or struggling with or even trying to numb out, we do not have to assign them the title of CEO. Emotions don't get to rule our every decision.

THURSDAY _____

FRIDAY _____

SATURDAY/SUNDAY _____

○ _____
○ _____
○ _____
○ _____
○ _____
○ _____
○ _____
○ _____
○ _____
○ _____
○ _____
○ _____
○ _____
○ _____
○ _____
○ _____
○ _____
○ _____
○ _____
○ _____

WEEK OF

ACTION STEPS FOR MY MISSION

○ _____

_____

_____

○ _____

_____

_____

○ _____

_____

_____

○ _____

_____

_____

MONDAY _____

TUESDAY _____

WEDNESDAY _____

Jesus invites, welcomes, and encourages everyone—the weak, the miserable, the overwhelmed, the hopeless, the tired—to 'come' to Him.

THURSDAY _____

FRIDAY _____

SATURDAY/SUNDAY _____

TO-DO LIST

○ _____
○ _____
○ _____
○ _____
○ _____
○ _____
○ _____
○ _____
○ _____
○ _____
○ _____
○ _____
○ _____
○ _____
○ _____
○ _____
○ _____
○ _____
○ _____

WEEK OF

○ _____

_____

○ _____

_____

○ _____

_____

○ _____

_____

MONDAY _____

TUESDAY _____

WEDNESDAY _____

When we feel overwhelmed, unhinged, or faint of heart, we cast our cares on Jesus.

THURSDAY _____

FRIDAY _____

SATURDAY/SUNDAY _____

TO-DO LIST

- ○ _____
- ○ _____
- ○ _____
- ○ _____
- ○ _____
- ○ _____
- ○ _____
- ○ _____
- ○ _____
- ○ _____
- ○ _____
- ○ _____
- ○ _____
- ○ _____
- ○ _____
- ○ _____
- ○ _____
- ○ _____
- ○ _____
- ○ _____
- ○ _____

WEEK OF _____

ACTION STEPS FOR MY MISSION

○ _____

_____

○ _____

_____

○ _____

_____

○ _____

_____

MONDAY _____

TUESDAY _____

WEDNESDAY _____

There is nothing neutral about living a mission-possible life.

TO-DO LIST

THURSDAY _____

FRIDAY _____

SATURDAY/SUNDAY _____

WEEK OF

MONDAY _____

ACTION STEPS FOR MY MISSION

○ _____

_____

○ _____

_____

○ _____

_____

○ _____

_____

TUESDAY _____

WEDNESDAY _____

138

There's power in the details.
There's purpose in being prepared.

THURSDAY _____

FRIDAY _____

SATURDAY/SUNDAY _____

- ◯ _____
- ◯ _____
- ◯ _____
- ◯ _____
- ◯ _____
- ◯ _____
- ◯ _____
- ◯ _____
- ◯ _____
- ◯ _____
- ◯ _____
- ◯ _____
- ◯ _____
- ◯ _____
- ◯ _____
- ◯ _____
- ◯ _____
- ◯ _____
- ◯ _____
- ◯ _____

REVIEWING THE PAST MONTH

WHAT WAS SUCCESSFUL THIS PAST MONTH:

MY WINS THIS PAST MONTH:

WHAT I DID THIS PAST MONTH TO FULFILL MY MISSION STATEMENT:

"LIVING MISSION POSSIBLE MEANS LIVING WITH AN ETERNAL MINDSIGHT, KNOWING THAT OUR WORK ON EARTH IS TO ACCOMPLISH SOMETHING OF ETERNAL VALUE."

WHAT I WANT TO CONTINUE TO FOCUS ON NEXT MONTH:

HOW GOD SHOWED HIMSELF TO ME THIS PAST MONTH:

_____
_____
_____
_____
_____
_____

3 THINGS I WILL DO

TO WORK TOWARD ACCOMPLISHING THE GOALS:

1 _____

_____

_____

2 _____

_____

_____

3 _____

_____

A PROMISE OF GOD

I WANT TO FOCUS ON THIS MONTH:

_____
_____
_____
_____
_____
_____
_____
_____

"

God will generously provide all you need. Then you will always have everything you
need and plenty left over to share with others. — 2 CORINTHIANS 9:8 (NLT)

MONTH

SUNDAY	MONDAY	TUESDAY

WEDNESDAY	THURSDAY	FRIDAY	SATURDAY

WEEK OF

ACTION STEPS FOR MY MISSION

○ _____

_____

_____

○ _____

_____

_____

○ _____

_____

_____

○ _____

_____

_____

MONDAY _____

TUESDAY _____

WEDNESDAY _____

A work ethic is pointless without a purpose. Working hard is not the end goal; we work hard to get to the end goal.

THURSDAY _____

FRIDAY _____

SATURDAY/SUNDAY _____

TO-DO LIST

○ _____
○ _____
○ _____
○ _____
○ _____
○ _____
○ _____
○ _____
○ _____
○ _____
○ _____
○ _____
○ _____
○ _____
○ _____
○ _____
○ _____
○ _____
○ _____
○ _____
○ _____

VERSE OF THE WEEK

ACTION STEPS FOR MY MISSION

○ _____

_____

_____

○ _____

_____

_____

○ _____

_____

_____

○ _____

_____

MONDAY _____

TUESDAY _____

WEDNESDAY _____

When you are committed to a mission, nothing can stop you.

TO-DO LIST

- ◯ _____
- ◯ _____
- ◯ _____
- ◯ _____
- ◯ _____
- ◯ _____
- ◯ _____
- ◯ _____
- ◯ _____
- ◯ _____
- ◯ _____
- ◯ _____
- ◯ _____
- ◯ _____
- ◯ _____
- ◯ _____
- ◯ _____
- ◯ _____
- ◯ _____
- ◯ _____
- ◯ _____

THURSDAY _____

FRIDAY _____

SATURDAY/SUNDAY _____

VERSE OF THE WEEK

ACTION STEPS FOR MY MISSION

○ _____

_____

○ _____

_____

○ _____

_____

○ _____

_____

MONDAY _____

TUESDAY _____

WEDNESDAY _____

As you wait for wisdom, an answer to prayer, or even healing, if you allow Him to, God will always position you to be used for His glory.

TO-DO LIST

THURSDAY _____

FRIDAY _____

SATURDAY/SUNDAY _____

WEEK OF _____

ACTION STEPS FOR MY MISSION

○ _____

_____

_____

○ _____

_____

○ _____

_____

○ _____

_____

MONDAY _____

TUESDAY _____

WEDNESDAY _____

We may not hold the power of foresight, but we have the power of choice. We can choose our attitude. We can choose where we deposit our hope. We can choose in what or whom we trust.

THURSDAY _____

FRIDAY _____

SATURDAY/SUNDAY _____

TO-DO LIST

○ _____
○ _____
○ _____
○ _____
○ _____
○ _____
○ _____
○ _____
○ _____
○ _____
○ _____
○ _____
○ _____
○ _____
○ _____
○ _____
○ _____
○ _____
○ _____
○ _____
○ _____

VERSE OF THE WEEK

WEEK OF

MONDAY _____

ACTION STEPS FOR MY MISSION

○ _____

_____

○ _____

_____

○ _____

_____

○ _____

_____

TUESDAY _____

WEDNESDAY _____

Will you make the choice to begin to see what's mission possible when you trust in Jesus?

TO-DO LIST

○ _____
○ _____
○ _____
○ _____
○ _____
○ _____
○ _____
○ _____
○ _____
○ _____
○ _____
○ _____
○ _____
○ _____
○ _____
○ _____
○ _____
○ _____
○ _____
○ _____
○ _____

THURSDAY _____

FRIDAY _____

SATURDAY/SUNDAY _____

REVIEWING THE PAST MONTH

WHAT WAS SUCCESSFUL THIS PAST MONTH:

MY WINS THIS PAST MONTH:

WHAT I DID THIS PAST MONTH TO FULFILL MY MISSION STATEMENT:

"THE SIGNIFICANCE YOUR LIFE CREATES CARRIES MORE VALUE THAN WHAT OTHERS THINK ABOUT YOU."

WHAT I WANT TO CONTINUE TO FOCUS ON NEXT MONTH:

HOW GOD SHOWED HIMSELF TO ME THIS PAST MONTH:

GOALS FOR THE UPCOMING MONTH

_____

_____

_____

_____

_____

_____

_____

_____

_____

_____

3 THINGS I WILL DO

TO WORK TOWARD ACCOMPLISHING THE GOALS:

1 _____

_____

_____

2 _____

_____

_____

3 _____

_____

_____

A PROMISE OF GOD

I WANT TO FOCUS ON THIS MONTH:

_____

_____

_____

_____

_____

_____

_____

_____

_____

_____

Rejoice in the Lord always; again I will say, rejoice! — PHILIPPIANS 4:4

MONTH

SUNDAY	MONDAY	TUESDAY

WEDNESDAY	THURSDAY	FRIDAY	SATURDAY

WEEK OF _____

ACTION STEPS FOR MY MISSION

○ _____

_____

○ _____

_____

○ _____

_____

○ _____

_____

MONDAY _____

TUESDAY _____

WEDNESDAY _____

Because of Jesus, namely His death and resurrection, we have the hope and the glory of living not for the temporary but for what's eternal.

THURSDAY _____

FRIDAY _____

SATURDAY/SUNDAY _____

TO-DO LIST

- ○ _____
- ○ _____
- ○ _____
- ○ _____
- ○ _____
- ○ _____
- ○ _____
- ○ _____
- ○ _____
- ○ _____
- ○ _____
- ○ _____
- ○ _____
- ○ _____
- ○ _____
- ○ _____
- ○ _____
- ○ _____
- ○ _____
- ○ _____

VERSE OF THE WEEK

ACTION STEPS FOR MY MISSION

○ _____

_____

_____

○ _____

_____

○ _____

_____

○ _____

_____

MONDAY _____

TUESDAY _____

WEDNESDAY _____

If we live for the here and now, of course we're going to focus on success and fun and living our best life now. . . . But, as the Bible tells us, this isn't our home.

THURSDAY _____

FRIDAY _____

SATURDAY/SUNDAY _____

TO-DO LIST

○ _____
○ _____
○ _____
○ _____
○ _____
○ _____
○ _____
○ _____
○ _____
○ _____
○ _____
○ _____
○ _____
○ _____
○ _____
○ _____
○ _____
○ _____
○ _____
○ _____

WEEK OF _____

MONDAY _____

TUESDAY _____

WEDNESDAY _____

ACTION STEPS FOR MY MISSION

○ _____

_____

○ _____

_____

○ _____

_____

○ _____

_____

Don't give up the mission because you don't fully understand it and can't figure out the game plan. . . . Remember what God has done in the past.

THURSDAY _____

FRIDAY _____

SATURDAY/SUNDAY _____

○ _____
○ _____
○ _____
○ _____
○ _____
○ _____
○ _____
○ _____
○ _____
○ _____
○ _____
○ _____
○ _____
○ _____
○ _____
○ _____
○ _____
○ _____
○ _____
○ _____

WEEK OF

ACTION STEPS FOR MY MISSION

○ _____

_____

○ _____

_____

○ _____

_____

○ _____

_____

MONDAY _____

TUESDAY _____

WEDNESDAY _____

We serve the God of this universe, who holds life itself in His hands.

TO-DO LIST

- ○ _____
- ○ _____
- ○ _____
- ○ _____
- ○ _____
- ○ _____
- ○ _____
- ○ _____
- ○ _____
- ○ _____
- ○ _____
- ○ _____
- ○ _____
- ○ _____
- ○ _____
- ○ _____
- ○ _____
- ○ _____
- ○ _____
- ○ _____

THURSDAY _____

FRIDAY _____

SATURDAY/SUNDAY _____

VERSE OF THE WEEK

ACTION STEPS FOR MY MISSION

○ _____

_____

○ _____

_____

○ _____

_____

○ _____

_____

WEEK OF _____

MONDAY _____

TUESDAY _____

WEDNESDAY _____

God is in this with you. He is beside you. He is rooting for you, and He is fighting for you.

TO-DO LIST

○ _____
○ _____
○ _____
○ _____
○ _____
○ _____
○ _____
○ _____
○ _____
○ _____
○ _____
○ _____
○ _____
○ _____
○ _____
○ _____
○ _____
○ _____
○ _____
○ _____
○ _____

THURSDAY _____

FRIDAY _____

SATURDAY/SUNDAY _____

REVIEWING THE PAST MONTH

WHAT WAS SUCCESSFUL THIS PAST MONTH:

MY WINS THIS PAST MONTH:

WHAT I DID THIS PAST MONTH TO FULFILL MY MISSION STATEMENT:

"WHEN YOU DETERMINE TO LIVE MISSION POSSIBLE, REST ASSURED YOU WILL NOT LOOK BACK ONE DAY AND WRESTLE WITH REGRET OR PAINFULLY WONDER WHAT YOU DID WITH YOUR LIFE."

WHAT I WANT TO CONTINUE TO FOCUS ON NEXT MONTH:

HOW GOD SHOWED HIMSELF TO ME THIS PAST MONTH:

GOALS FOR THE UPCOMING MONTH

_____

_____

_____

_____

_____

3 THINGS I WILL DO

TO WORK TOWARD ACCOMPLISHING THE GOALS:

1 _____

_____

2 _____

_____

3 _____

_____

A PROMISE OF GOD

I WANT TO FOCUS ON THIS MONTH:

_____

_____

_____

_____

_____

_____

_____

66

The Lord is my strength and my song;
He has become my salvation. — PSALM 118:14 (HCSB)

MONTH

SUNDAY	MONDAY	TUESDAY

WEDNESDAY	THURSDAY	FRIDAY	SATURDAY

WEEK OF

ACTION STEPS FOR MY MISSION

○ _____

_____

_____

○ _____

_____

_____

○ _____

_____

_____

○ _____

_____

MONDAY _____

TUESDAY _____

WEDNESDAY _____

Start small. Don't obsess about changing the world.
Start by changing one person.

THURSDAY _____

FRIDAY _____

SATURDAY/SUNDAY _____

○ _____
○ _____
○ _____
○ _____
○ _____
○ _____
○ _____
○ _____
○ _____
○ _____
○ _____
○ _____
○ _____
○ _____
○ _____
○ _____
○ _____
○ _____
○ _____
○ _____

WEEK OF _____

ACTION STEPS FOR MY MISSION

○ _____

_____

○ _____

_____

○ _____

_____

○ _____

_____

MONDAY _____

TUESDAY _____

WEDNESDAY _____

A mission-possible life is often marked by miracles.

TO-DO LIST

THURSDAY _____

FRIDAY _____

SATURDAY/SUNDAY _____

WEEK OF _____

ACTION STEPS FOR MY MISSION

○ _____

_____

_____

○ _____

_____

_____

○ _____

_____

_____

○ _____

_____

_____

MONDAY _____

TUESDAY _____

WEDNESDAY _____

We can do something difficult and uncomfortable that stretches us and doesn't feel good, because we know there are greater gains.

THURSDAY _____

FRIDAY _____

SATURDAY/SUNDAY _____

○ _____
○ _____
○ _____
○ _____
○ _____
○ _____
○ _____
○ _____
○ _____
○ _____
○ _____
○ _____
○ _____
○ _____
○ _____
○ _____
○ _____
○ _____
○ _____
○ _____

VERSE OF THE WEEK

ACTION STEPS FOR MY MISSION

○ _____

_____

_____

○ _____

_____

_____

○ _____

_____

_____

○ _____

_____

_____

MONDAY _____

TUESDAY _____

WEDNESDAY _____

When you flip your perspective on the uncomfortable, you may find that a setback can look a lot more like a setup.

THURSDAY _____

FRIDAY _____

SATURDAY/SUNDAY _____

TO-DO LIST

○ _____
○ _____
○ _____
○ _____
○ _____
○ _____
○ _____
○ _____
○ _____
○ _____
○ _____
○ _____
○ _____
○ _____
○ _____
○ _____
○ _____
○ _____
○ _____
○ _____

VERSE OF THE WEEK

ACTION STEPS FOR MY MISSION

○ _____

_____

_____

○ _____

_____

_____

○ _____

_____

_____

○ _____

_____

_____

MONDAY _____

TUESDAY _____

WEDNESDAY _____

God has a purpose and a plan for my life and for each and every person on this earth.

TO-DO LIST

○ _____
○ _____
○ _____
○ _____
○ _____
○ _____
○ _____
○ _____
○ _____
○ _____
○ _____
○ _____
○ _____
○ _____
○ _____
○ _____
○ _____
○ _____
○ _____
○ _____
○ _____

THURSDAY _____

FRIDAY _____

SATURDAY/SUNDAY _____

MY MISSION-POSSIBLE YEAR IN REVIEW!

IF YOU COULD DESCRIBE THE PAST YEAR IN ONE WORD, WHAT WOULD IT BE?

WRITE OUT YOUR MISSION STATEMENT FROM THE BEGINNING OF THE YEAR:

WHAT WERE SOME WINS FROM THE PAST YEAR? BIG OR SMALL—CELEBRATE THEM!

WRITE OUT HOW YOU LIVED OUT SOME OR ALL OF YOUR MISSION STATEMENT:

HOW DID GOD SHOW HIMSELF TO YOU THESE PAST TWELVE MONTHS?

WHAT ARE YOU DREAMING AND PRAYING ABOUT FOR THE NEXT YEAR?

NOTES

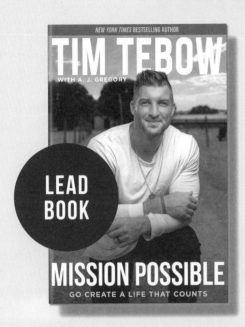
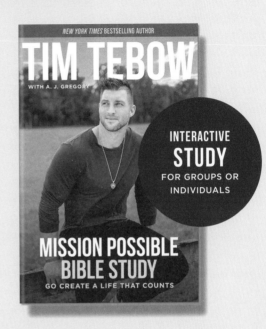
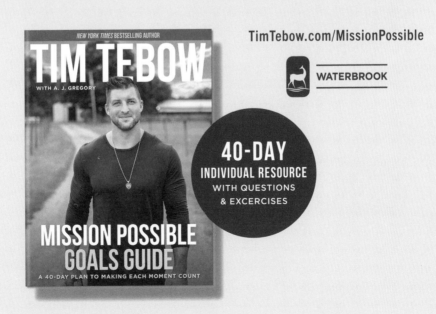

NEW YORK TIMES BESTSELLER
TIM TEBOW
WITH A. J. GREGORY
THIS IS THE DAY
Reclaim Your Dream. Ignite Your Passion. Live Your Purpose.

TIM TEBOW
NEW YORK TIMES BESTSELLER
SHAKEN
DISCOVERING YOUR TRUE IDENTITY IN THE MIDST OF LIFE'S STORMS
WITH A.J. GREGORY

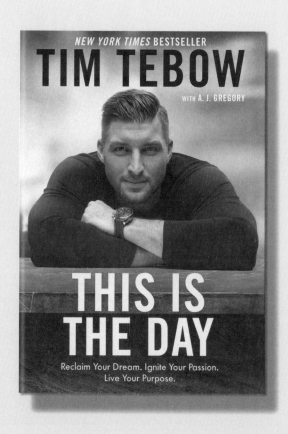

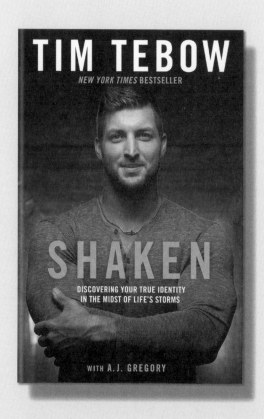

MORE FROM TIM TEBOW!

TIM TEBOW'S KIDS' BOOKS!

Tim Tebow
A Party to Remember
BRONCO AND FRIENDS
A Party to Remember
New York Times Bestseller
Tim Tebow
with A. J. Gregory illustrated by Jane Chapman

Tim Tebow
BRONCO AND FRIENDS
Mission Possible
WATERBROOK
BRONCO AND FRIENDS
Mission Possible
New York Times Bestselling Author
Tim Tebow
with A. J. Gregory illustrated by Jane Chapman

TimTebow.com/MissionPossible

WATERBROOK

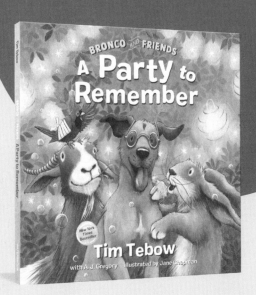

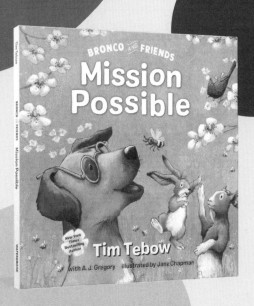

MISSION POSSIBLE WEEKLY PLANNER

All Scripture quotations, unless otherwise indicated, are taken from the New American Standard Bible®, copyright © 1960, 1962, 1963, 1968, 1971, 1972, 1973, 1975, 1977, 1995 by the Lockman Foundation. Used by permission. (Lockman.org). Scripture quotations marked (HCSB) are taken from the Holman Christian Standard Bible®, copyright © 1999, 2000, 2002, 2003, 2009 by Holman Bible Publishers. Used by permission. Holman Christian Standard Bible®, Holman CSB®, and HCSB® are federally registered trademarks of Holman Bible Publishers. Scripture quotations marked (NIV) are taken from the Holy Bible, New International Version®, NIV®. Copyright © 1973, 1978, 1984, 2011 by Biblica Inc.™ Used by permission of Zondervan. All rights reserved worldwide. (zondervan.com). The "NIV" and "New International Version" are trademarks registered in the United States Patent and Trademark Office by Biblica Inc.™ Scripture quotations marked (NLT) are taken from the Holy Bible, New Living Translation, copyright © 1996, 2004, 2015 by Tyndale House Foundation. Used by permission of Tyndale House Publishers, a division of Tyndale House Ministries, Carol Stream, Illinois 60188. All rights reserved.

Hardcover ISBN 978-0-593-19410-2

Published in the United States by WaterBrook, an imprint of Random House, a division of Penguin Random House.

WaterBrook® and its deer colophon are registered trademarks of Penguin Random House LLC.

Printed in Malaysia

waterbrookmultnomah.com

2022—First Edition

10 9 8 7 6 5 4 3 2 1

SPECIAL SALES
Most WaterBrook books are available at special quantity discounts when purchased in bulk by corporations, organizations, and special-interest groups. Custom imprinting or excerpting can also be done to fit special needs. For information, please e-mail specialmarketscms@ penguinrandomhouse.com.